WONDERING TO BETHLEHEM

A Wonder-Filled
Advent Devotional for Kids

Vanessa Myers

Wondering to Bethlehem: A Wonder-Filled Advent Devotional for Kids

WHAT PEOPLE ARE SAYING ABOUT WONDERING TO BETHLEHEM...

"In *Wondering to Bethlehem*, Vanessa gives all of us permission to slow and experience the Christmas story with fresh eyes. We get to ask all the questions we always wanted to ask (or didn't know we had permission to ask), and unpack all the wonders embedded at the heart of our glorious gospel. Yes, this is a children's devotional, but it will make the Christmas story come alive for the whole family."

-- Rev. Carolyn Moore
Lead Pastor at Mosaic Church Evans, Podcaster at The Art of Holiness,
Author of *When Women Lead, Supernatural, Encounter the Father,*
Encounter Jesus, Encounter the Spirit, & The 19.

"Pack your bags for a curiosity-filled adventure! *Wondering to Bethlehem* will have your kids thinking about aspects of Jesus' birth story they never knew they were allowed to wonder about before. Teach your kids to think past just the bare facts and truly engage their creative thinking skills to help the familiar story become fresh and alive."

-- Christie Thomas
Award-winning author of *Fruit Full: 100 Family Experiences*
for Growing in the Fruit of the Spirit

"I love how simply written, yet thought-provoking, *Wondering to Bethlehem* is for children. Using our imaginations to "wonder" through the Christmas story brings renewed excitement and joy to the season. Every family should take the opportunity to do this wonderful devotional together. I have a feeling that parents may get as much, if not more, out of wondering through this wonderful devotion."

-- Donnie Slade
President/CEO of Kidz Blitz Ministries

"*Wondering to Bethlehem* gives families many beautiful ways to approach the beloved account of Jesus' birth. It helps cultivate persistent curiosity about the people and emotions of the story, deeper understanding of the biblical events, and joyful worship in response to all the Lord has done."

-- Valerie Ellis

Author of *Share the Joy! A Christmas Lift-the-Flap Book* and Founder of oureverydayparables.com

"Wondering helps kids not only develop imagination but also can help them develop emotional vocabulary and empathy. *Wondering to Bethlehem* encourages kids to identify with the emotions and faith stories of the people involved in the story of the birth of Jesus. This devotional is a great resource for parents to not only lead their kids through Advent but also develop the emotional vocabulary and empathy needed for healthy relationships."

-- Michelle Nietert, M.A., LPC-S

Clinical Director of Hope Helps, Author of 6 books including *Managing Your Emojis* and the Bringing Big Emotions to a Bigger God series including *God, I Feel Sad/Scared*.

"What a great tool for families as they journey into the Advent season. Vanessa's wondering questions had me picturing families having those same conversations as they walked through this daily devotional."

-- Christy Slade

Merch Director, Kidz Blitz Ministries

For Lyla, Maverick, Remy, and Mary Belén,
May you be filled with wonder and joy every Christmas as
you remember the birth of our Savior, Jesus Christ.

TABLE OF CONTENTS

Introduction   9

Passport Information   13

1. Can I Take It Back?   14

2. Gabriel Visits Mary   18

3. Troubling Words   22

4. How Will This Be?   26

5. A Loud Voice   30

6. Sing It, Mary!   34

7. What's He Going to Be?   38

8. Zechariah's Song   42

9. The Family Tree of Jesus   46

10. Joseph Wants to Divorce Mary   50

11. Joseph's Dream   54

12. Old Testament Prophecy   58

13. Joseph Obeyed   62

14. Time to Count the People   66

15. No Vacancy   70

16. Swaddling Cloths   74

17. The First Announcement   78

18. The Angels Praise God   82

19. The First Christmas Rush 86

20. Start Spreading the News 90

21. A Mother's Pondering 94

22. Praise the Lord 98

23. Simeon Holds the Messiah 102

24. Anna Shares About Jesus 106

Suitcase Stickers 110

Bonus Devotions 111

Is He Here Yet? (Christmas Day) 112

The Star Has Risen (Epiphany) 116

Notes 120

Acknowledgments 123

About the Author 125

INTRODUCTION

● ● ● ● ● ● ● ● ● ● ● ● ●

I wonder...

Have you ever said those words after reading a story in the Bible?

When I read the Bible, I like to read between the lines - what else was going on during the story? I love details, and my mind always begins to wonder about what might have been going on that the Bible doesn't tell us.

When you are reading the Bible, it is important to look for wisdom and knowledge about God. He wants us to learn about Jesus and how to live as Christians, and we need knowledge about God in order to share about Him with others.

But God also gave us imagination and wonder. Our God is an imaginative God! Look around at His Creation and you will see just how big His imagination is! You will see the wonder in all the details of every living thing. It is so amazing!

In this book, I want you to use both knowledge and wonder as you begin your journey to Bethlehem and to the birth of our Savior, Jesus Christ. I want you to read the Bible (along with the devotions) so that you can gain knowledge, but I also want you to use your wonder and imagination to go beyond the things that you already know about the birth of Jesus and think deeper about the story. I want you to use your senses as you read and really imagine what else might have been in the scene. What kind of smells might there have been? What would things have felt like? What sounds could have been surrounding the characters? What could the

9

characters have been thinking? Use your imagination and senses to really develop the true wonder of the Christmas story.

Get Your Passport Ready!

Wondering to Bethlehem is a journey you will be taking with Mary and Joseph, from the town of Nazareth to the town of Bethlehem. It's a journey of wondering and imagination! During this journey, you will document your travels through every story. To do that, you will be creating a passport throughout this book, filling the pages with all the stories of the Bible you have wondered to along your journey and using your imagination as you read.

Before your wondering begins, make sure you fill out the Passport Information page and draw a picture of yourself (or snap a photo of yourself, print it out, and paste it into the book). Every traveler must have a picture of themselves! After every devotion, you will find a Wondering Notes page. On this page you will write down things you are wondering about in the story for the day, draw a picture of the story in the Wondering Snapshot box, and then enjoy the Wonders to Unpack, which involves something cool about the story, plus you can mark your journey with a sticker. To download the stickers, use the QR code found on the next page and then print them out onto round labels (or you can print on regular paper and glue them into the book).

Let's answer some questions now that you might be wondering about before we begin our journey...

What is Advent?

Advent is the first season of the year for the Christian church, beginning four Sundays before Christmas and ending on Christmas Eve. The word Advent means "coming," as during this season Christians prepare for the coming of Christ.

How Do I Use this Devotional?

The beginning of Advent differs every year since it always begins four Sundays before Christmas. Most Advent calendars or readings you will find use December 1-24 as the celebration of Advent. For this devotional, you will begin your readings on December 1st and end on Christmas Eve, December 24th. I have also included two bonus devotions to be read on Christmas Day (December 25th), and on Epiphany (January 6th, the day we celebrate the arrival of the Magi).

Let's Wonder!

Are you ready? Got your bags packed? Have your mind all set to use your wonder and imagination? Excited to learn more about the Christmas story? Let's begin our journey and our Wondering to Bethlehem!

TO DOWNLOAD THE PASSPORT STICKERS,

SCAN HERE

Use Avery 2" Round Labels for printing (I used #22817)

PASSPORT INFORMATION

Name ————————————

Date of Birth ——————————

Country————————————

Draw a picture of yourself!

CAN I TAKE IT BACK?
LUKE 1:5-25

"Zechariah asked the angel, 'How can I be sure of this? I am an old man and my wife is well along in years.'" Luke 1:18

Have you ever said something and immediately wished you could take it back?

I am wondering if this is how Zechariah, a priest, felt after his encounter with the angel Gabriel.

Zechariah and his wife, Elizabeth, were faithful followers of God. They were devoted to Him and desired to be obedient to God in everything. But when it came time for God to do something amazing for them, Zechariah questioned the Lord.

Zechariah had been chosen to enter the temple to burn incense. During this time, while others were outside the temple praying, the angel Gabriel appeared to Zechariah and told him something shocking that might cause you to react in the same way he did.

Gabriel told him that Elizabeth (who was very old and could not have children) would give birth to a son. God had heard their prayers and would bless them, giving them a son that they were to name John. He would be the one that would prepare the way for the Lord Jesus. He would tell everyone that the Messiah, the One who had been promised by God, was coming soon!

After this amazing news you would think that Zechariah would have jumped for joy, but instead, he questioned what the angel told him because of how old he and Elizabeth were. Because of this doubt, he was not able to speak for the entire nine months that Elizabeth was pregnant.

There is so much inside this story that has my imagination swirling! Here are some things I wonder about in this story:

- I wonder exactly how old Zechariah and Elizabeth were when John was born?
- I wonder if Zechariah screamed out in fear when Gabriel appeared to him?
- I wonder why this priest, who was full of faith in God, did not believe at first?
- I wonder if Zechariah wished he would not have questioned God's message to him?
- I wonder if Elizabeth got upset with her husband for questioning what the angel said?
- I wonder what it was like for Zechariah not to be able to speak for nine months?

God sent a special message to this married couple. He would use their son to tell others about Jesus. This miracle of a baby would help others come to know who Jesus was: the Savior of the world. John would "bring back many of the people of Israel to the Lord their God" (Luke 1:16). Talk about a wonder!

Thank You, Lord, for the wonder of this story. Thank You for using John to tell others about You. Help me boldly share about You with others, just like John did. Amen.

WONDERING NOTES

• • • • • • • • • • • • •

Things I wonder about in this story...

_____

_____

_____

_____

WONDERING SNAPSHOT

Draw a picture of the story

WONDERS TO UNPACK

● ● ● ● ● ● ● ● ● ● ● ● ● ●

Gabriel's message from God to Zechariah was the first time God had spoken to the Israelites in 400 years! The last time God spoke to them was recorded in Malachi 4:5-6. After that, there were 400 years of silence - no messages from God. But this message to Zechariah from God broke the silence! John was the sign that Jesus - the Messiah, the Savior of the world - was coming!

Place Day 1 Sticker Here

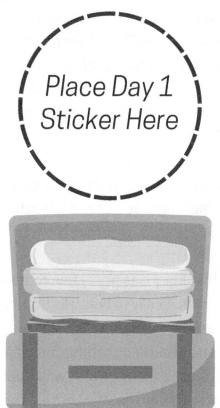

2

GABRIEL VISITS MARY
LUKE 1:26-28

"The angel went to her and said, 'Greetings, you who are highly favored! The Lord is with you.'" Luke 1:28

Six months have passed since our last story. And guess who shows up again? The angel Gabriel!

This time the angel pays a visit to a young girl from Nazareth named Mary, who was pledged to be married to a man named Joseph - a descendant of King David (*this piece of information is important to know for future reference in our wonderings*).

Why would Gabriel go to a small town in Galilee and appear to a young girl? Because Gabriel had an important message to share with her from the Lord!

What Gabriel was about to share with her would rock her world, bringing her a message that would change her life. In order for Mary to clearly hear this message, Gabriel had to tell her two things before the message was delivered: that she was favored by God and that the Lord was with her.

The first thing - that Mary was highly favored by God – meant that God chose her specifically to bring His Son into this world. He would use her to be the mother of Jesus. Mary needed to know that she was chosen by God and that this message from Gabriel was the real deal. It wasn't fake news - it was true!

Secondly, Gabriel told Mary that the Lord was with her. If you're visited by an angel who was about to deliver life changing news, I think you would want to be reminded of God's presence with you! God needed Mary to know these two important things before delivering His message to her.

So, put yourself in this moment with Mary. What do you think would be going through her head? What do you wonder about in this specific moment before Gabriel drops this important message from God on her? Here are some of my wonderings:

- I wonder where Mary was in Nazareth at the time of Gabriel's visit? Was she at home or out and about in the town?
- I wonder what Mary was doing at that specific moment when Gabriel appeared? Was she cooking, folding clothes, or doing other chores?
- I wonder why God chose Mary?
- I wonder how strong Mary's faith was in God?

As you think about these few verses, I want you to remember that God calls you favored and loved by Him too. I want you to remember that God is always with you. No matter what goes on in your life, keep these two messages from God to Mary at the front of your mind. You are favored by God and He is with you!

Heavenly Father, remind me daily of Your love and Your presence with me. Amen.

WONDERING NOTES

Things I wonder about in this story...

_____

_____

_____

_____

WONDERING SNAPSHOT

Draw a picture of the story

WONDERS TO UNPACK

• • • • • • • • • • • • •

We do not know the exact age of Mary when she was visited by the angel Gabriel, but we do know that Jewish girls married young at this time in history. This means that Mary was more than likely a teenager when Gabriel appeared to her.

Place Day 2
Sticker Here

3

TROUBLING WORDS
LUKE 1:29-33

"Mary was greatly troubled at his words and wondered what
kind of greeting this might be." Luke 1:29

One Christmas when my kids were younger, we surprised them
with a trip to Disney World! They had no idea they would be leaving
on a trip the next day for a fun vacation! And you want to know
what was funny? Both of my girls reacted in opposite ways! My
oldest was jumping up and down and screaming with excitement,
but my youngest just sat there. No reaction at all. Almost like the
words we just said troubled her. Was she even excited about
going?

I believe Mary reacted in the same way my youngest daughter
did when the angel Gabriel came to visit her to deliver some very
unexpected news. Remember in yesterday's devotion, Gabriel said
Mary was favored and that God was with her. And her reaction to
Gabriel's words is found in verse 29, where she was "greatly
troubled at his words and wondered what kind of greeting this
might be." Is this the same reaction you might have had?

First of all, not many people are visited by an angel, so Mary had
to be in shock. When the angel told her that she was favored and
that God was with her, she honestly didn't know how to react. I can
just picture Mary standing there, mouth open, with no reaction.

But I love how the Bible says that Mary "wondered." Her brain
was spinning. Perhaps she was wondering some of these things:

- Why did the angel come to visit me?
- Why am I favored by God?
- Why did God choose me?
- Why did Gabriel greet me this way?
- Why is this happening to me?

And then Gabriel tells her the most amazing news: she is going to bring God's Son into the world! He is going to be Great, the Son of the Most High, a King that would rule forever. And she is to give Him the name Jesus! *(Cue the boom, mic drop, or whatever sound you want to make when such powerful news is delivered).*

This news was incredible! But Mary's initial reaction, I believe, was one of shock and not knowing how to react - like she was in utter disbelief that this was even happening to her.

After asking my youngest daughter why she reacted the way she did with the Disney World news, she said she wasn't sure we were telling the truth, almost like we were pulling a fast one on her or like that moment wasn't even real.

Did Mary initially feel the same way? I wonder...

Holy God, thank You for giving Your Son Jesus to be our Savior. I pray for any friends who have not accepted this wonderful news of Jesus to find Your love this Christmas season. Amen.

WONDERING NOTES

● ● ● ● ● ● ● ● ● ● ● ●

Things I wonder about in this story...

_____

_____

_____

_____

WONDERING SNAPSHOT

Draw a picture of the story

WONDERS TO UNPACK

● ● ● ● ● ● ● ● ● ● ● ● ●

The name Mary means "beloved," or someone who is dearly loved. And what a great reminder to Mary that God chose her because she is dearly loved and favored by Him.

Place Day 3
Sticker Here

4

HOW WILL THIS BE?
LUKE 1:34-38

"'How will this be,' Mary asked the angel, 'since I am a virgin?'"
Luke 1:34

Remember our very first devotion when Gabriel came to visit Zechariah and he questioned the angel's news? His response was, "How can I be sure of this?" (Luke 1:18). Because of his unbelief, he was not able to speak for nine months while his wife, Elizabeth, was pregnant with their son, John.

When Gabriel came to visit Mary, she asked a similar question but with a little bit of a different take. She asked, "How will this be?" (Luke 1:34). I am certain that Mary had no doubt in her mind about what the angel had just told her. I know she believed that what Gabriel said would come true. But she was human (and we like to know things), so she asked Gabriel how she would be able to bring God's Son into the world. How was it going to happen?

"The Holy Spirit will come on you, and the power of the Most High will overshadow you. So the holy one to be born will be called the Son of God" (Luke 1:35).

The answer she received is that it will happen when the Holy Spirit comes over her and God's power overshadows her (the Amplified Bible says overshadowing is like a cloud coming over you). I don't know if Mary was expecting that kind of answer or not, but what powerful words!

Gabriel also threw in there that Elizabeth (Zechariah's wife who happens to be a relative of Mary), was six months pregnant in her old age. That might have also been news to Mary, as Elizabeth and Zechariah had been living away from people for the first five months of her pregnancy with John (Luke 1:24). This means that Mary probably didn't even know Elizabeth was pregnant. Gabriel was showing Mary that God had already done one awesome wonder…and now He was going to do the best wonder ever!

As I begin to wonder about these few verses of the story, here are some things that pop into my mind:

- I wonder if Mary fully understood what was going to happen?
- I wonder if Mary had more questions but was too afraid to ask?
- I wonder if Mary was scared at all?
- I wonder why Zechariah and Elizabeth didn't go out for the first five months that she was pregnant with John?

Mary took this all in and accepted this message from God. She said, "May your word to me be fulfilled" (Luke 1:38). What a strong faith Mary had!

Powerful God, give
me the faith of Mary
and help me to always
believe in Your Word.
Amen.

WONDERING NOTES

● ● ● ● ● ● ● ● ● ● ● ● ●

Things I wonder about in this story...

_____

_____

_____

_____

WONDERING SNAPSHOT

Draw a picture of the story

WONDERS TO UNPACK

There was one more point that Gabriel wanted to make in the message to Mary, an important thing to remember: "For no word from God will ever fail" (Luke 1:37). Gabriel wanted to make sure Mary understood that God never fails. He always does what He says He's going to do. Remember that!

Place Day 4 Sticker Here

5

A LOUD VOICE
LUKE 1:39-45

"In a loud voice she exclaimed: 'Blessed are you among women, and blessed is the child you will bear!'" Luke 1:42

Ask my family, the kids at my church, or the friends I sit with at my kids' soccer games if I am quiet or loud and they will all tell you - I am definitely LOUD! I love to smile, talk to people, and be cheerful, so I guess that spills out of me and I tend to be loud. And when I get excited about something, I usually get even louder!

Someone in our story likes to be loud when she gets excited too. And that would be Elizabeth, Mary's relative!

After the angel Gabriel visited Mary to tell her she was going to give birth to God's Son, she quickly left and went to see her relative, Elizabeth (remember Elizabeth is pregnant with John, who is the one that will tell others that the Messiah is coming). As soon as she enters Zechariah and Elizabeth's house and speaks, Elizabeth feels little baby John inside her tummy do a leap! John recognized the voice of the woman who was carrying God's Son!

This fills Elizabeth with so much joy and excitement that she shouts out loud, "Blessed are you among women, and blessed is the child you will bear!" (Luke 1:42). Isn't it amazing that Elizabeth immediately knew about the child Mary was carrying? Mary hadn't even said anything to her about it yet. Elizabeth knew just by the presence and voice of Mary, as well as baby John leaping in her womb.

This story fills me with so much wonder and joy that tears well up in my eyes. I can only imagine what that moment would have felt like between these two women.

- I wonder if Mary and Elizabeth jumped up and down and screamed with excitement?
- I wonder if Elizabeth gave her any advice about what it would be like to be pregnant?
- I wonder if Zechariah and Mary exchanged details about their visits from Gabriel?

But my favorite part of this story is what Elizabeth says to Mary in verse 45, "Blessed is she who has believed that the Lord would fulfill his promises to her!" Mary is blessed because she BELIEVED the Lord. She believed the message that Gabriel delivered. She believed that God would bring His Son into this world through her. She believed.

I pray that you will believe, just as Mary did. I pray that you will believe that Jesus is your Savior. I pray that you will accept Him into your life and obey His Word. I pray that you will believe with all your heart that He loves you no matter what. I pray that you, like Mary, believe.

Almighty God, help me to always believe in You. Remind me daily of Your presence and Your love for me. Amen.

WONDERING NOTES

Things I wonder about in this story...

_____

_____

_____

_____

WONDERING SNAPSHOT

Draw a picture of the story

WONDERS TO UNPACK

Luke 1:15 says that John will be "filled with the Holy Spirit even before he is born." This moment when Mary arrives was most likely the point in which John became filled with the Holy Spirit.

Place Day 5 Sticker Here

6

SING IT, MARY!

LUKE 1:46-56

"And Mary said: 'My soul glorifies the Lord and my spirit rejoices in God my Savior.'" Luke 1:46-47

I have some wonderful friends who are a very musical family. All four of them can sing and play instruments. They are very talented! What I love about the two teenagers in the family is how they just burst out in song wherever they are. They don't care who is around, they just sing it loud! And I love that! If I'm around them when they do this, then I like to join in and sing loud with them (even though I'm not much of a singer)!

After Elizabeth greeted Mary and told her she was blessed, I believe Mary was so moved and filled with the Holy Spirit that she burst into song. For me, when I am so moved and filled with the Spirit, I like to sing too! Mary and I have something in common!

Mary's song was one of praise to God for what He was doing through her. She praised the Lord for many things: for seeing her, for calling her blessed and favored, for doing great things for her, for being holy, for showing mercy to everyone, for performing mighty deeds, for bringing down evil rulers and lifting up those who are humble, for filling those who are hungry for Him with good things, and for keeping His promises. So many things to praise God for!

I love how she didn't hold back. She wasn't shy about singing praises to God in front of Elizabeth. She didn't care who was around. She just sang her heart out in praise to her Almighty God.

I like to wonder what this moment was like for Mary:

- I wonder if Mary sang quietly or loudly?
- I wonder if the song was slow or fast?
- I wonder if Mary lifted up her hands in praise as she sang to God?
- I wonder if Elizabeth closed her eyes and worshiped right along with Mary?
- I wonder if little baby John continued to leap in the womb as Mary sang?

What I want you to take away from this story is that Mary worshiped the Lord and praised Him. She didn't care who was around. She just sang and lifted her voice to praise the Lord.

I know what you're thinking...because I see it every Sunday morning when I lead worship songs with my church kids. You look around and see who else is singing before you start singing. You don't want to be embarrassed if you are the only one singing that praise song to the Lord, so if no one else is singing, you don't want to either. But I challenge you to throw all that shyness out the window and worship God. Just sing. Don't worry about what others think. It's a moment between you and the Lord. Let's sing to the Lord, just like Mary did!

Holy God, help me not to be afraid to sing praises to You. Fill my heart with joy and wonder so that it bursts out of me in praise to You. Amen.

WONDERING NOTES

● ● ● ● ● ● ● ● ● ● ● ●

Things I wonder about in this story...

_____

_____

_____

_____

WONDERING SNAPSHOT

Draw a picture of the story

WONDERS TO UNPACK

This song of Mary's is known as "The Magnificat" because all she wanted to do was magnify God's name and not her own. She wanted to make His name great!

Place Day 6
Sticker Here

7

WHAT'S HE GOING TO BE?
LUKE 1:57-66

"Everyone who heard this wondered about it, asking, 'What then is this child going to be?' For the Lord's hand was with him." Luke 1:66

What do you want to be when you grow up? When I was young, I wanted to be a teacher. I would "play school" at my house and pretend like I was in charge of my own classroom. My mom was a teacher, so I used to take her old workbooks and lay them out on my bedroom floor, pretending they were my students' desks. Because I wanted to be a teacher when I grew up, I enjoyed playing school! And I am a teacher today, but just not in a school. Instead, I teach in the church!

We all have big dreams and plans for things we want to do in our lives. When you were born, your parents may have even wondered about what you would grow up to be.

But I know a set of parents who didn't have to wonder what their son would be. They knew the plans God had for him!

It soon came time for Elizabeth to give birth to her son, John. He was the child the angel Gabriel had told Zechariah would be the one to prepare the way of the Lord and lead Israel back to Him. The one who would tell others that the Savior was coming. They knew how great this child would be because God had delivered a message to them telling them so.

Eight days after John was born, he was circumcised and given his name (as was the Jewish tradition). When asked his name,

Elizabeth said his name was to be John. They didn't believe her, so they asked Zechariah, who grabbed a pen and paper and wrote down the name John. And it was at that moment he was able to speak again!

The friends and neighbors with them witnessed this miracle of Zechariah receiving his voice back, and they knew something was special about this child. That got their minds wondering…who will this child be? What does God have in store for this little baby?

As I really think about this story, I have some of my own wonderings:

- I wonder if Elizabeth got frustrated with the others when they questioned the name she gave to her baby?
- I wonder if Elizabeth was so happy when she finally got to hear her husband's voice after a long nine months?
- I wonder if the friends and neighbors who witnessed this grew deeper in their faith in God because of it?

Elizabeth and Zechariah knew the plans God had for their son, John. They knew John would do great things because the angel had told them so. They may not have truly grasped how big a part their son would play in the birth of Jesus and in His ministry on Earth, but in that moment after John's birth, I believe Elizabeth and Zechariah had peace because they knew what their son would grow up to be.

Awesome God, thank You for using John to pave the way for Jesus. Guide my life and lead me on the path to the plans You have for me. Amen.

WONDERING NOTES

● ● ● ● ● ● ● ● ● ● ● ● ●

Things I wonder about in this story...

_____

_____

_____

_____

WONDERING SNAPSHOT

Draw a picture of the story

WONDERS TO UNPACK

● ● ● ● ● ● ● ● ● ● ● ● ●

In Jewish tradition, males were typically named after their father. But Elizabeth and Zechariah chose not to follow tradition and instead listened to the Lord, naming him John just as God had said to.

Place Day 7 Sticker Here

DRAW A PICTURE OF...

Zechariah	Elizabeth	John

8

ZECHARIAH'S SONG
LUKE 1:67-80

"Praise be to the Lord, the God of Israel, because he has come
to his people and redeemed them." Luke 1:68

What would be the first thing you would say after nine months of
not being able to speak? Maybe you would give thanks for the
return of your voice, talk to your parents, tell a joke, call your best
friend, sing a song, or maybe even repeat the same thing over and
over again just to hear your own voice.

Remember, Zechariah had been unable to speak since his visit
from the angel Gabriel, where he doubted the news that he and his
wife would be able to have a child in their old age. It had been nine
months of not being able to talk out loud to his wife, his friends,
and his fellow priests.

So, you know what the first thing out of Zechariah's mouth was
when God restored his voice?

A song of praise to God!

He had witnessed the birth of his child eight days before, and
now it was time to give him the name that God had said. Zechariah
obeyed God, and because of his obedience, his voice was restored!

Zechariah was filled with the Holy Spirit and broke out into song.
In this song, he prophesied (telling of what is to come in the future)
about Jesus. He praised God for sending His Son to redeem us (by
taking on our sins and dying on the cross for us so we could live
forever in heaven with God), for giving us salvation from our

enemies, for showing us mercy, for rescuing us, and for being able to serve Him without fear. He then goes on and sings over John, delivering such beautiful words of what John will do to prepare the way for Jesus.

I often wonder what this moment was like for Zechariah...

- I wonder if Zechariah screamed and shouted when he was praising God?
- I wonder if, after hearing his voice return, he cried?
- I wonder if he picked up his son, John, as he sang?
- I wonder if his friends praised God right along with him?

God had given Zechariah and Elizabeth a miracle in the birth of John. Two elderly people were blessed by God with a child. I can only imagine the overwhelming joy and blessing they felt because of what God had done for them, and for what God would use their son to do as well.

So, the next time God blesses you with something, what if you choose to give praise to God before you do anything else? If you want to follow Zechariah's example, you can sing a song of praise for His blessing!

God of All, thank You for the many blessings You give to me. Help me to always praise Your name and give thanks to You. Amen.

WONDERING NOTES

● ● ● ● ● ● ● ● ● ● ● ●

Things I wonder about in this story...

_____

_____

_____

_____

WONDERING SNAPSHOT

Draw a picture of the story

WONDERS TO UNPACK

John grew up in the wilderness until he began his public ministry (Luke 1:80). He waited patiently until God called him out of the wilderness and into his ministry to Israel when he was around 30 years old. This is the same age Jesus was when He began His public ministry (remember John and Jesus were only six months apart in age).

Place Day 8 Sticker Here

45

9

THE FAMILY TREE OF JESUS
MATTHEW 1:1-17

"And Jacob the father of Joseph, the husband of Mary, and
Mary was the mother of Jesus who is called the Messiah."
Matthew 1:16

It's time to be honest! How many of you looked up this Scripture
passage in Matthew 1 and skimmed over it? How many of you
looked at it and decided not to read it at all?

There are so many names in this chapter and most of them are
hard to pronounce, so why is it important to read this list of
names?

Because it's the family tree of Jesus! And because it holds some
very well-known and important names from the Old Testament!

Matthew was one of Jesus's twelve disciples, and in his book, he
records the life of Jesus. He starts by listing a bunch of names
that are just too hard to say, but he did this, I think, for a very good
reason.

You see, back in those days, it was very important for Jewish
people to know their lineage (where they came from). And it was
especially important to know your family tree if you were claiming
to be the Son of David (which is King David who conquered the
giant, Goliath). Jesus made this claim that He was the Son of David
- and He is!

One thing I love about this family tree (or what is also called the
genealogy of Jesus), is looking at some of the people who are
listed here. Take a look at the passage and write down some

names that you recognize from the Old Testament.

Maybe you recognize the names Abraham, Isaac, Jacob, Judah, Boaz, King David, or King Solomon. Or maybe even the names of the four women: Tamar, Rahab, Ruth, or Uriah's wife (Bathsheba). Those are the names of some very cool people! And Jesus was descended from them!

What kinds of things are you wondering right now about this list of names? Here is what is going through my mind:

- I wonder if Abraham could have ever imagined that the Son of God would come from his family?
- I wonder if Rahab ever thought about how great an impact her decision to help the Israelite spies would turn out to be? (See Joshua 2)
- I wonder if Ruth ever thought she would one day be the great-grandmother of a king? And from him, descend the greatest King in history?
- I wonder who all these other people are (whose names I can't pronounce very well)?

I think it's absolutely amazing to look back at the family tree of Jesus and see the people in His family. So, go back now and reread this passage. It doesn't matter how you pronounce the names. Just say them out loud and be amazed by the family tree of Jesus.

Creator God, thank You for using these people in Jesus's family tree to help others come to know You. Use me to tell others about You too. Amen.

WONDERING NOTES

● ● ● ● ● ● ● ● ● ● ● ● ●

Things I wonder about in this story...

_____

_____

_____

_____

WONDERING SNAPSHOT

Draw a picture of the story

WONDERS TO UNPACK

In the Old Testament, prophets foretold that the Messiah would be born of a virgin (Isaiah 7:14), that He would be from the descendants of Abraham (Genesis 22:18), that He would be from the tribe of Judah (Genesis 49:10), and that He would come from the family of David (2 Samuel 7:12-13).[1] Pretty cool, right?

Place Day 9 Sticker Here

10

JOSEPH WANTS TO DIVORCE MARY

MATTHEW 1:18-19

"Because Joseph her husband was faithful to the law, and yet did not want to expose her to public disgrace, he had in mind to divorce her quietly." Matthew 1:19

Do you want to know something about Joseph that I learned from this passage?

He was a good man with a heart filled with love for people and love for the Lord. And because of this love, he wanted to do right by Mary.

Joseph was pledged to be married to Mary (some versions of the Bible say he was "betrothed" to Mary). It was like being engaged in today's terms, except the difference was that being betrothed was like being already married (whereas being engaged in our day isn't being married yet). There was a legal agreement between the man and woman that made the relationship binding. There would still be a marriage ceremony, but being betrothed meant you were going to marry that person and no one else. So, in order to get out of this betrothal, you would have had to get a divorce.

Sounds kind of complicated, right?

Remember, the angel Gabriel told Mary that she was going to give birth to the Son of God and name Him Jesus. When Joseph found out that she was pregnant with a child (who was not his child), he wanted to do the only thing he knew to do. He had to divorce Mary.

But he was a good man. He didn't want to embarrass Mary and make a big public display about this. Because you see, Mary would have been very humiliated and seen as an outcast in her community. Joseph had a lot of love and respect for Mary, so he wanted to divorce her quietly.

As I think about these few verses, my mind wonders...

- I wonder how Mary told Joseph that she was pregnant?
- I wonder at what point she told Joseph that she was pregnant? She had been at Elizabeth's house for three months, so did she wait until she got home from there to tell him?
- I wonder if Joseph thought she was crazy and didn't believe her when she told him?
- I wonder if Joseph was really upset when he learned this news?
- I wonder if Mary cried when she knew Joseph wanted to divorce her?

Joseph was delivered some very hard news, which I am sure made him feel angry, sad, confused, and hurt. He didn't understand. But those feelings of wanting to divorce Mary quietly didn't last long. Wait until tomorrow when we find out what made Joseph change his mind about divorcing Mary...

Almighty God, when life hits us with hard news, help us to turn to You for comfort and guidance. Amen.

WONDERING NOTES

● ● ● ● ● ● ● ● ● ● ● ● ●

Things I wonder about in this story...

_____

_____

_____

_____

WONDERING SNAPSHOT

Draw a picture of the story

WONDERS TO UNPACK

At that time in history, if a man divorced his wife, it meant the man would still receive all the money that the woman's father gave to her for the marriage.[2] In wanting to divorce her quietly (not in court), Joseph showed that he cared more about Mary than he did about money. Joseph was a good man!

Place Day 10 Sticker Here

JOSEPH'S DREAM
MATTHEW 1:20-21

"Joseph, son of David, do not be afraid to take Mary home as your wife, because what is conceived in her is from the Holy Spirit." Matthew 1:20b

Joseph was in a tough spot. The woman he had planned to marry was pregnant with a child that was not his. But he loved Mary and didn't want to disgrace her, so he chose to divorce her quietly. He had a plan, but while he was still thinking it through, God intervened and changed Joseph's mind.

And guess how God chose to speak to Joseph? In a dream!

In this dream, an angel of the Lord came to visit Joseph. The angel told him not to be afraid to take Mary as his wife.

Let's stop right there for a second. I just want to point out how amazing it was that God knew exactly the words that Joseph needed to hear. He knew that Joseph was afraid of going through with the marriage to Mary. He knew that Joseph was afraid of how this would look to other people. He knew that Joseph was afraid of how this would affect Mary. God knew. And so, God chose to speak to Joseph through an angel in a dream. So awesome!

The angel continued to share with Joseph that Mary is favored by God, that the baby inside her is from the Holy Spirit and is God's Son, and that this baby is the Savior that God promised long ago. He is the One who will come to take away the sins of the world. He is the One who will save the people. And His name will be Jesus.

I love that the angel told Joseph the exact same thing that Mary was told. There was no difference. The angel told them both not to be afraid, that the baby would be from the Holy Spirit, that the baby would be God's Son, that the baby would save people from their sins, and that they were to give Him the name Jesus. Isn't it so cool that God delivered the same message to them both?

As I sit and think about this story some more, I wonder…

- I wonder how many months Mary had been pregnant when the angel visited Joseph?
- I wonder if Joseph's stomach was in knots as he thought about divorcing Mary quietly?
- I wonder what Joseph's reaction was in his dream when the angel came to visit him? Was he in awe?
- I wonder if Joseph felt peace after he woke up from his dream?
- I wonder if he told anyone else about the dream from God?

Joseph was afraid of all that had happened with Mary. I am thinking that he totally didn't expect anything like this to happen to him. He had to feel some disappointment in what was happening. But then he had a dream, and all those fears were washed away. Praise be to God!

Holy God, thank You for sending Your angel to tell Joseph of Your plan for this baby. Help me to listen to You. Amen.

WONDERING NOTES

● ● ● ● ● ● ● ● ● ● ● ● ●

Things I wonder about in this story...

_____

_____

_____

_____

Draw a picture of the story

WONDERS TO UNPACK

● ● ● ● ● ● ● ● ● ● ● ● ● ● ●

The name "Jesus" comes from the name "Joshua" (Yeshua in Hebrew). It means "God is Salvation," or "Savior." Jesus came to save all people from their sins. He is our Savior!

Place Day 11 Sticker Here

12

OLD TESTAMENT PROPHECY
MATTHEW 1:22-23

"All this took place to fulfill what the Lord had said through the prophet: 'The virgin will conceive and give birth to a son, and they will call him Immanuel' (which means 'God with us')." Matthew 1:22-23

When God speaks about something, it will happen. And that is Truth. We can see this is true just from reading the Bible passage for today.

Joseph was visited by an angel of the Lord who told him that the baby Mary was carrying was from the Holy Spirit, and that He would save people from their sins.

Our verses today point us to the book of Isaiah in the Old Testament. Verse 23 is what God spoke to the prophet Isaiah about Jesus. This prophecy (foretelling what is to come) happened 700 years before the birth of Jesus. That's a long time, right?

The Jewish people knew of this prophecy, as it had been told to them throughout the generations. They had been waiting for it to come true for a very long time. Some of them probably had given up hope that God was going to bring this Savior into the world. But everything God says will come true.

Let's compare Matthew 1:23 and Isaiah 7:14 and you will see that God's prophecy is about to happen...

- The virgin is going to have a baby (Mary)
- She will give birth to a son (baby boy Jesus)
- His name will be Immanuel (which means God with us)

Now, wait a minute. The angel said that His name would be Jesus, but these two verses say that His name will be Immanuel (some Bible versions spell it like Emmanuel). Why are there two different names for this baby?

Well, guess what? Jesus has many names! Jesus is His name, but another name He is also called is Immanuel, or "God with us." When God came to the Earth in the form of a baby boy named Jesus, He was with us, giving special meaning to the name. So amazing!

I can only begin to imagine what might have been happening in the minds of Joseph and the Jewish people...

- I wonder if anyone else believed Mary and Joseph when they said their baby was God's Son?
- I wonder why it took 700 years for God to bring Jesus into the world?
- I wonder how many Jews had given up hope, or how many Jews still believed that what God had said would come true?

Things may not happen in the time frame we would like for them to, but if God speaks, you better believe it will happen.

Almighty God, thank You for telling Your people what was to come. Help me to continue to have faith in You. Amen.

WONDERING NOTES

Things I wonder about in this story...

_____

_____

_____

_____

WONDERING SNAPSHOT

Draw a picture of the story

WONDERS TO UNPACK

Want to know more names of Jesus? Read Isaiah 9:6 and you will find that Jesus is also called these names: Wonderful Counselor, Mighty God, Everlasting Father, Prince of Peace.

Place Day 12 Sticker Here

13

JOSEPH OBEYED
MATTHEW 1:24-25

"When Joseph woke up, he did what the angel of the Lord had commanded him and took Mary home as his wife."
Matthew 1:24

How hard do you find it to obey your parents? Or to obey your teacher at school? Or even to obey your pastor or small group leaders at church?

Showing complete obedience to those in authority over us can sometimes be hard. Because let's be honest, we only want to do what we want to do. But your parents, teachers, and pastors are there to guide you, teach you, and lead you in the path of the Lord.

What about being obedient to God? Do you find that hard to do? I do! Sometimes what God says is hard to do and I just don't want to do it. Sometimes I think that I know better than God (which is totally not true), and sometimes I just don't feel like doing what God wants me to do.

I am so thankful for the examples we have in the Bible of people showing complete obedience to God. In today's story, that person is Joseph.

After Joseph woke up from his dream where an angel of the Lord told him about who Jesus was, the Bible says that he obeyed God. He didn't partially obey God. He fully and completely obeyed God. He didn't wait around and think about it some more. He woke up and did what the Lord had commanded him to do.

Joseph went home, got Mary, and took her as his wife. They got married! He obeyed what the Lord said. After the baby was born, he obeyed God again by giving Him the name Jesus. There was no debating what name to give Him. This Son of God already had a name. I'm so thankful that both Joseph and Mary followed exactly what God had told them to do.

What do I wonder about in this story?

- I wonder if Mary was surprised when Joseph came home and said that God had spoken to him in a dream?
- I wonder if Joseph got excited when he was telling Mary about his dream and what the angel had said to him?
- I wonder if Mary finished Joseph's sentence with the name Jesus when he said, "And we have to name the baby..."
- I wonder what life was like for the two of them during those nine months of Mary being pregnant with the Son of God?
- I wonder if people looked down upon them or if people showed them kindness and love?

God speaks to us in many different ways: through people, creation, dreams, songs, road signs, and emails. But no matter how God speaks to us, we must obey what He says. Because we know that He is good, we know that what He says is also good and that He knows what is best for us.

Gracious God, help me to listen and obey You, just like Joseph did. Amen.

WONDERING NOTES

• • • • • • • • • • • •

Things I wonder about in this story...

_____

_____

_____

_____

WONDERING SNAPSHOT

Draw a picture of the story

WONDERS TO UNPACK

Joseph obeyed God because he was a faithful Jewish man who loved God and knew the Old Testament prophecies about the birth of a Savior. After the angel's visit in his dream, Joseph knew that this baby was from God, and he obeyed everything the Lord asked him to do.

Place Day 13
Sticker Here

14

TIME TO COUNT THE PEOPLE
LUKE 2:1-5

"In those days Caesar Augustus issued a decree that a census should be taken of the entire Roman world." Luke 2:1

How many people do you have in your family that live in your house? Go ahead and count them out loud. Now that you have counted, do you think it's necessary to tell someone in the government how many people live in your house?

Actually, it is! It's what is called a census. In America, our government takes a census every ten years. Your family fills out paperwork that answers questions about how many people live in your household. The census helps with keeping track of how many people live in a country *(side note…in the 2020 census of the United States of America, there were 331,449,281 people living in our country)*.[3]

In the days of the birth of Jesus, Caesar Augustus made it a law that all people in the Roman Empire should be counted in a census. For this census, the Roman government required each male to return to their hometown so that their name, occupation, property, and family could be recorded.[4]

This meant that Joseph and Mary had to do this around the same time that Jesus was to be born. They were living in Nazareth at the time, but they had to travel to Bethlehem to take part in the census because Joseph was descended from the line of King David, and David was from the city of Bethlehem. Nazareth isn't exactly close to Bethlehem though. There is a distance of about 90 miles between these two cities. Given that Mary was very pregnant, the journey could have taken up to a week. Who wants to travel by foot (or donkey) for 90 miles when you're about to have a baby? No one! I can only begin to wonder what was going through their minds when they found out about the census...

- I wonder if Mary was upset when she learned that she would have to travel a long way right around the time of Jesus's birth?
- I wonder what they packed for their journey?
- I wonder if there were things that she forgot at home that she wished she would have brought with her?
- I wonder if Mary's parents were sad that she was leaving her hometown so close to giving birth?

Want to hear something cool though? The prophet Micah prophesied that Jesus would be born in Bethlehem. Go read Micah 5:2 in the Old Testament. God told the people that the Greatest Ruler would come out of Bethlehem, and that Ruler is Jesus! One more cool thing is how God used Caesar Augustus - the emperor of Rome - and his decision to create a law for a census as a way of taking Joseph and Mary to the birthplace of Jesus. God's hand is everywhere and in everything. Praise be to God!

Heavenly Father, I love to see how the story of the birth of Jesus is found in the Old Testament and how everything You said came true. Thank You for bringing us Jesus, our Savior! Amen.

67

WONDERING NOTES

● ● ● ● ● ● ● ● ● ● ● ●

Things I wonder about in this story...

_____

_____

_____

_____

WONDERING SNAPSHOT

Draw a picture of the story

WONDERS TO UNPACK

Jesus was born in Bethlehem. The name "Bethlehem" means "house of bread." One of the names of Jesus is "Bread of Life" (John 6:35). How cool that the Bread of Life was born in a city called the house of bread!

Place Day 14
Sticker Here

15

NO VACANCY
LUKE 2:6-7

> "While they were there, the time came for the baby to be born, and she gave birth to her firstborn, a son. She wrapped him in cloths and placed him in a manger, because there was no guest room available for them." Luke 2:6-7

When I was growing up, there was one thing I always remembered about hotels: the vacancy sign. Each hotel I can recall had a large sign outside by the road advertising their hotel name, along with a neon sign underneath it that said "Vacancy" or "No Vacancy." Vacancy meant that there was space for travelers and rooms available that you could rent for the night. No Vacancy meant that there were no rooms available, so you would have to find another place to stay.

When Mary and Joseph finally arrived in the town of Bethlehem, after a very long and hard road trip on foot (or by donkey), there were no hotels. No large neon signs to announce if they had room or not for the night. In the book of Luke, it says there was "no guest room available for them" (Luke 2:7b). A guest room more than likely refers to a place in someone's home, probably that of a relative. Remember Joseph had to come back to Bethlehem for the census because this was his hometown. So more than likely he had relatives still living there.

But it seems that all rooms were occupied on the night they arrived. So, they were forced to stay in a place where animals likely stayed. Our tradition today calls it a stable (because that's where we keep farm animals), but people back then kept animals in caves.

So, let's use our imagination to think about what it might have been like for Mary and Joseph inside this cave...

- I wonder if it smelled really bad?
- I wonder if they had to be careful where they walked so they didn't step in animal poop?
- I wonder if Mary cried when they learned there was no guest room available for them to stay?
- I wonder if Mary got mad that she had to give birth to a baby in a place where animals were kept?
- I wonder if Joseph gave her a big hug and told her that everything would be ok?

There was no room for Mary and Joseph that night. No guest room for baby Jesus to be born in. No fancy hotel. No beds. Not even a door. But it was the right place for God's Son to be born. A lowly place for a humble King to enter the world.

Most Holy God, thank You for providing just the right place for the birth of Jesus. Even though it probably wasn't what Mary and Joseph were expecting, it was what You had planned, and it was perfect. Thank You, Lord. Amen.

71

WONDERING NOTES

Things I wonder about in this story...

_____

_____

_____

_____

WONDERING SNAPSHOT

Draw a picture of the story

WONDERS TO UNPACK

I recently learned that shepherds would herd their sheep into caves at night and light a campfire at the entrance to the cave to keep the sheep inside and safe.[5] This cave that held the Savior was probably filled with black walls and soot from the fire as well as animal poop, which probably caused it to smell really bad in there.

Place Day 15 Sticker Here

16

SWADDLING CLOTHS
LUKE 2:6-7

"And she gave birth to her firstborn, a son. She wrapped him in cloths and placed him in a manger, because there was no guest room available for them." Luke 2:7

Just recently, a friend of mine had a baby and she sent me the sweetest photo. Her baby girl was all wrapped up in a blanket with a big bow on her head. The only part of the baby that you could see was her head. Her legs and arms were all tucked snuggly inside the blanket.

Have you ever wondered why we wrap babies in blankets when they are born?

Blankets for newborns are best if they are used as a swaddling blanket. Swaddling is a particular way of wrapping a blanket around a baby, folding the blanket tightly around a baby's body (everything but the head). This style of blanket wrapping keeps babies calm, soothed, warm, and helps them to sleep better.

Did you know that mothers back at this time in history wrapped their babies in a blanket too? However, they weren't called blankets back then. In our Bible verse today, it uses the word "cloths." Other translations of the Bible say "swaddling cloths" or "bands of cloth." These bands of cloth were long, and mothers used them to give the arms and legs of their baby strength, protection, and to assure proper growth.[6]

After settling into the cave, the time came for Jesus to be born. After Jesus was born, Mary took these bands of cloth and wrapped

Jesus up. Then, as the Scripture says, she laid Him in a manger.

So, what exactly is a manger? It's a feeding trough for animals! Most mangers you see in our Nativity scenes are made of wood, but back then, mangers were actually made from stone. If you want to see what one looks like, just go online with your parents and search for stone mangers. You'll find plenty of pictures of what one looks like. Doesn't look very comfy for a newborn baby though!

Now that you know what the birthplace of Jesus was like, what are you wondering about?

- I wonder how many swaddling cloths Mary packed for the trip to Bethlehem?
- I wonder if Mary wished she had a better bed for baby Jesus to lay in?
- I wonder if the animals laid near the manger because they somehow knew that this baby was special?

Close your eyes and picture the scene we have just discussed: a cave that is dark, smelly animals, a stone trough for a bed, a newborn baby swaddled in bands of cloth, and two parents filled with love for this baby who is God's Son. Not the picture we would expect for the birth of the Savior of the world, but it's exactly what God had planned.

Amazing Lord, thank You for swaddling cloths and stone troughs. Thank You for providing for us in unexpected ways every day, just as You did when Jesus was born. Amen.

WONDERING NOTES

Things I wonder about in this story...

_____

_____

_____

_____

WONDERING SNAPSHOT

Draw a picture of the story

WONDERS TO UNPACK

Jesus being born in a cave where animals were kept showed that Mary and Joseph were most likely poor. Had they been rich, a room would probably have been available for them. But Jesus was born in this lowly place to help us understand that He came to save ALL people. Not just the rich, but the poor too. He came for everyone.

Place Day 16 Sticker Here

17

THE FIRST ANNOUNCEMENT
LUKE 2:8-12

"But the angel said to them, 'Do not be afraid. I bring you good news
that will cause great joy for all the people. Today in the town of David
a Savior has been born to you; he is the Messiah, the Lord.'"
Luke 2:10-11

Let's imagine this scene for a minute:

You're a shepherd near the town of Bethlehem. Your job is taking care of a flock of sheep. It's not a glamorous job. Not a job that makes a lot of money. It's actually one of the poorest jobs in the country of Israel.

It's nighttime and you're out in the fields taking care of your sheep. You're not sleeping either. You are watching your sheep, making sure they are safe while they sleep and aren't in danger from other animals.

Things are really quiet. It's very peaceful at night as you tend to your flock and watch over them. Then out of nowhere, an angel of the Lord appears to you and this bright light shines all around you. Nothing like this has ever happened before, so at first you are afraid. Actually, you're terrified. What is happening?

But then, the angel begins to speak in a calm voice and tells you not to be afraid. The angel delivers good news, which will bring great joy for all people: the Savior has been born in Bethlehem. The Savior that God promised is finally here! And then the angel goes on to say that you will know Him when you find Him, wrapped in bands of cloth and lying in a manger. Now that is some exciting news!

Let's dive a little deeper into our imaginations and wonder some more things about this story...

- I wonder how many shepherds there were in the field that night?
- I wonder how many sheep were in the field with them?
- I wonder if any of the shepherds screamed when the first angel appeared out of nowhere?
- I wonder if they were wondering why an angel appeared to them to tell them this news? Why them and not someone else?
- I wonder if they wanted to ask the angel questions about the Savior's birth? Did they want more details about where to find Him?

The fact that God chose to deliver the news to shepherds first is amazing! God brought this news to them to show that He came for everyone. Also, shepherds were men who were not easily fooled. They were practical and reliable.[7] If they told you something, you could believe them. I love that God used shepherds to make the first announcement of Jesus's birth to the world!

Almighty God, I love how You used simple people to deliver a powerful message. May I always remember that Your Son was born to save all people. Amen.

WONDERING NOTES

● ● ● ● ● ● ● ● ● ● ● ● ●

Things I wonder about in this story...

_____

_____

_____

_____

WONDERING SNAPSHOT

Draw a picture of the story

WONDERS TO UNPACK

When the angels announced the birth of Jesus to the shepherds, it was the first time in centuries that the glory of God (or the presence of God) had appeared on Earth. The last time had been when the glory of God was present in the temple that King Solomon had built. God's glory departed right before the temple was destroyed by the Babylonians and the Israelites were exiled out of their country (see Ezekiel 10-11).

Place Day 17 Sticker Here

18

THE ANGELS PRAISE GOD
LUKE 2:13-14

"Glory to God in the highest heaven, and on earth peace to those on whom his favor rests." Luke 2:14

Let's go back to the field near Bethlehem, where the shepherds had just been visited by an angel of the Lord and were delivered the news about the birth of Jesus.

One angel had already terrified the shepherds (see Luke 2:9), and now something happened that probably made them jump back even farther in surprise - a multitude of angels appeared and started praising God!

Let's think about this. What does one angel praising God sound like? Beautiful for sure, but probably not extremely loud. However, when you get a multitude or a great company of heavenly hosts together, it's got to be loud, right? It's got to be the most glorious sound you have ever heard. It's got to be a moment in the life of these shepherds that they would never forget.

The angels said, "and on earth peace to those on whom his favor rests" (Luke 2:14). This message is for everyone to know that Jesus came to bring peace, that God was sending His Son - the Prince of Peace - to this earth so that we could have peace. And the angels praised God for this.

Some things I wonder about in this story...
- I wonder what the sheep did when all the angels appeared and a bright light shone around them?

- I wonder if anyone else around these fields outside of Bethlehem saw the bright light that shone around the shepherds? Was anyone else awake at that time of night to catch a glimpse of the brightness?
- I wonder exactly how many angels were in this "great company of the heavenly host" (Luke 2:13)?
- I wonder how loud their praises to God were?
- I wonder how long the praising lasted?
- I wonder if the shepherds joined in the praising?

The angels praised God for sending His Son to be born on the Earth. What do you praise God for? Make a list with your family of things to praise God for. Then, say them out loud together, and say them loudly so that the whole world can hear your praises!

Loving God, I praise You for all You have given to me and all that You do for me. I cannot thank You enough for Your many blessings in my life. Amen.

BORN
TO WORSHIP

WONDERING NOTES

Things I wonder about in this story...

_____

_____

_____

_____

WONDERING SNAPSHOT

Draw a picture of the story

WONDERS TO UNPACK

The angels praised God at the beginning of Creation (see Job 38:4-7). And now, the angels praised God at the beginning of a new creation: the birth of God's Son.[8]

Place Day 18 Sticker Here

19

THE FIRST CHRISTMAS RUSH
LUKE 2:15-16

"So they hurried off and found Mary and Joseph, and the baby, who was lying in the manger." Luke 2:16

Have you ever heard of a Christmas Rush? Maybe you have been part of one or perhaps your parents have been the ones in the thick of it.

A Christmas Rush is a time when lots of people begin their Christmas shopping, going from store to store in search of the greatest gifts for their friends and family. This usually happens closer to Christmas Day, as a lot of us tend to wait until the last minute to go shopping. You can tell when there's a Christmas Rush, as there are lots of people out shopping and a ton of traffic!

The very first Christmas Rush was nothing like we see today. But there was a group of people who rushed, not to buy the greatest gift, but to SEE the greatest gift ever given to us.

After the angels left them, the shepherds made a unanimous decision: we must go to Bethlehem to see this baby! They just had the most incredible experience with the visit from the angels. Nothing like they had ever seen. And they all agreed they HAD to go to Bethlehem!

The shepherds left their fields and went to Bethlehem, but we can see that it was a Christmas Rush based on the words found in verse 16. Depending on what translation of the Bible you are reading from, you might see phrases in verse 16 like "hurried off," "went with haste," or "they were running." No matter which words are used, we know that the shepherds did not wait around. They HAD to see this baby. They had to go to Bethlehem to find Joseph, Mary, and baby Jesus, who was lying in a manger. And they found Him!

As I sit here and picture this group of shepherds taking off for Bethlehem, my mind starts wondering…

- I wonder who they left the sheep with so that they could all go see baby Jesus? I know they didn't leave them unattended!
- I wonder if they were still in shock from what had just happened or if they were pumped up and excited?
- I wonder how long it took them to run to Bethlehem?
- I wonder how they knew where to look?
- I wonder if the angels gave them a few more details about where to look that were not recorded in the Bible?

The most important thing to notice in this story is that the shepherds didn't wait. They obeyed the angels and quickly went to find the Savior of the world. There was no waiting around and thinking it over. They believed and they knew that what the angels had said was true. And they had to go and see the gift that God had given to the world.

Thank You, Lord, for the quickness of the shepherds who obeyed and went to find baby Jesus. Help me to listen to You, just as the shepherds did. Amen.

WONDERING NOTES

• • • • • • • • • • • •

Things I wonder about in this story...

_____

_____

_____

_____

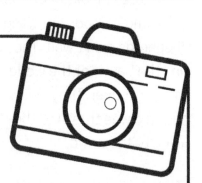

WONDERING SNAPSHOT

Draw a picture of the story

WONDERS TO UNPACK

Bethlehem is known as the City of David. Before David was a king, he had been a shepherd in Bethlehem. God sent shepherds to the City of David (who was a shepherd) to see The Good Shepherd (another name for Jesus), who had been born there. Isn't that cool?

Place Day 19
Sticker Here

20

START SPREADING THE NEWS
LUKE 2:17-18

"When they had seen him, they spread the word concerning what had been told them about this child." Luke 2:17

What do you do when you receive good news? You share it with others!

Maybe the good news that you want to share is about a new baby being born in your family, a new pet, an A you made on that math test that was so hard, a trip to Disney World, a favorite toy you found that had been lost for a while, or a new video game you got for your birthday that you had been wanting for a long time. Lots of good news to share with other people!

The shepherds were the first people to learn of the Good News about the birth of our Savior, Jesus Christ. The angels came to deliver the message to them and told them how they would know who the baby was. So, they quickly took off for Bethlehem and found Jesus lying in a manger, just as the angels had said.

I can just picture the shepherds bubbling over with so much excitement after seeing Jesus that they just had to share this news with other people. It was too great of an event to keep to themselves. Others needed to hear about it. So they started spreading the Good News!

They left the cave where Jesus lay and told others what had been told to them by the angels concerning this child and who He was. As I think more about this story, my mind begins to wonder…

- I wonder how long they stayed to visit with Mary and Joseph?
- I wonder if they told Mary and Joseph about their amazing visit from the angels?
- I wonder if they asked Mary if they could hold baby Jesus?
- I wonder if they shed some tears when they saw Him because this was the Son of God? (It would be hard for me NOT to cry.)
- I wonder who they went and told? Other family members? Friends? Random people they didn't know?
- I wonder if they woke people up and banged on their doors to tell them of this amazing news?

No matter what time of day it was when the shepherds told others the Good News of Jesus's birth, we know from the Bible that ALL were amazed (Luke 2:18). All of these people were Jewish, and they knew the prophecy that had been spoken by Isaiah 700 years ago. They knew that God had promised to send a Savior in the form of a baby. And now this baby was here, and they were all amazed!

Holy God, thank You for the Good News of Jesus's birth. Give me the boldness to share about who Jesus is with others, just like the shepherds did. Amen.

WONDERING NOTES

●　●　●　●　●　●　●　●　●　●　●　●　●

Things I wonder about in this story...

_____

_____

_____

_____

WONDERING SNAPSHOT

Draw a picture of the story

WONDERS TO UNPACK

After the shepherds finished spreading the Good News of Jesus's birth, guess what they did? They glorified and praised God, which is just what the angels did when they came to tell the shepherds the Good News!

Place Day 20 Sticker Here

21

A MOTHER'S PONDERING
LUKE 2:19

"But Mary treasured up all these things and pondered them in her heart." Luke 2:19

What do you do when you want to remember something in a way that you will never forget it? Maybe you want to remember something encouraging that your mom said to you, an amazing vacation that you took with your family, all of the details about winning that basketball championship, or even something that you read in the Bible or felt God say to you. So, what can you do to remember all these things?

I'll tell you my little secret…I write those memories down! I have lots of journals from when I was younger filled with memories of things that I did or said. As I have gotten older, I have realized that my memory doesn't work as well as it used to. So I am thankful that I took the time to write down special memories over my lifetime, whether that be in a journal or in a post on Facebook.

In our Bible verse today, we see Mary - a new mom - just sitting back, taking everything in. The verse says that she "treasured" and "pondered" the events surrounding Jesus's birth. Other translations of the Bible say she "remembered" or "kept" them. No matter what translation is read, we know that Mary is really thinking about all these things that have happened.

She has already experienced so much in these last nine months of being pregnant, and now she is overwhelmed with wonder and awe that God has brought His Son into the world through her. She not only had to give birth in a city that was not her own, but also in a cave where animals were kept. And now she's just been visited by shepherds who said that angels came to them in the fields at night and told them about the birth of Jesus. So many amazing things have happened, and she is making sure to store all these memories in her heart and really think about them.

What do you think Mary is wondering or pondering in her heart? Here are some of my wonderings:

- I wonder if Mary wrote any of these memories down?
- I wonder if she and Joseph talked about everything that had just happened?
- I wonder if, as she was treasuring and pondering these things, tears welled up in her eyes because of the wonder of what had just happened?
- I wonder if Mary had the biggest smile on her face as she took it all in?
- I wonder if Mary continually praised the Lord for what He had done?

If you want to remember something amazing that God has done in your life (whether it's big or small), write it down! Take the time to store up each memory in your heart by writing about it in a journal. One day you will be glad you did.

Loving God, help me to treasure Your words and hide them in my heart, just like Mary. Amen.

WONDERING NOTES

Things I wonder about in this story...

_____

_____

_____

_____

WONDERING SNAPSHOT

Draw a picture of the story

WONDERS TO UNPACK

We are not only to remember things that God has done for us, but should also think about, ponder, and remember what God has said to us in the Bible. When you read your Bible and want help in remembering its words, write the verses down. Fill a notebook with God's Word!

Place Day 21 Sticker Here

22

PRAISE THE LORD
LUKE 2:20

"The shepherds returned, glorifying and praising God for all the things they had heard and seen, which were just as they had been told." Luke 2:20

When God does something really cool in my life, you know what I like to do?

Tell people! I love to share with others how amazing God is! I get so excited to let people know all the details because God is so good! There is no one like Him!

But the first thing I do (or at least I try to do…sometimes I forget), is to praise the Lord. When something so awesome happens, I whisper a "Thank You, Jesus!" or a "Praise the Lord!" Whether it's a big thing or a small thing, I praise the Lord for it. Sometimes I might even start singing my favorite worship song in praise to Him.

After the shepherds found Mary and Joseph in that cave - with their new baby wrapped in swaddling cloths and lying in a manger - they went and told people all about what God had done. They couldn't wait to let others know about this amazing gift that God had just given to everyone. And the people they told were filled with awe and wonder.

After all that excitement, it was then time to go home. But the shepherds weren't sad about having to return to their jobs. They were filled with such wonder that they went home glorifying and praising God! I can just imagine them skipping or running home with big smiles on their faces, singing their hearts out in praise to God. I can just picture their joy - they were so happy!

The shepherds praised God because they had seen the Savior, God's Son, but they also praised God because what He had told them through the angels was true. Everything the angels had spoken to the shepherds happened just as they had been told. No detail was false. All truth!

As I imagine this part of the story in my mind, I begin to wonder...

- I wonder if people noticed a difference in the shepherds when they returned home? Were they more joyful than usual?
- I wonder if they prayed to God more than they had before?
- I wonder if their families' lives were changed by what they had heard and seen? Did their family members grow deeper in their faith in God because of what happened?

Our lives change when we see God work in mighty ways. Our faith is strengthened, and our hearts are filled with praise. Those are the times when it's easier to praise God. Things aren't always good, but that doesn't mean that God isn't good. He is always good! So, no matter if things are good or bad in your life, may you always remember to praise the Lord. His love for you and His presence in your life never changes.

Father God, help me to remember to praise You every day, no matter what. Amen.

WONDERING NOTES

● ● ● ● ● ● ● ● ● ● ● ●

Things I wonder about in this story...

_____

_____

_____

_____

WONDERING SNAPSHOT

Draw a picture of the story

WONDERS TO UNPACK

Even though Jesus is not here on Earth with us anymore, He sent the Holy Spirit to be with us. And it is the Holy Spirit that transforms our lives today. We can still have life changing experiences like the shepherds did through the Holy Spirit, and I am so very thankful for this!

Place Day 22 Sticker Here

23

SIMEON HOLDS THE MESSIAH
LUKE 2:21-35

"Moved by the Spirit, he went into the temple courts. When the
parents brought in the child Jesus to do for him what the custom of
the Law required, Simeon took him in his arms and praised God."
Luke 2:27-28

Have you ever held a newborn baby? If you have a baby brother or
sister, you probably have. They are so tiny, super cute, and very
snuggly. Newborn babies sleep a lot in the first few weeks of their
lives, so it's easier to hold them close and rock them. Maybe you
have gotten a chance to hold your little brother or sister as they
sleep and not when they are crying!

Forty days after the birth of Jesus, we find the only mention of
someone in the Bible (other than Mary and Joseph) who held baby
Jesus. And it was a promise fulfilled by God for a man named
Simeon.

Mary and Joseph were still in Bethlehem forty days after Jesus
was born. Because they were devout Jewish people, they followed
the Jewish customs and laws for what to do after a baby's birth
(which are found in Leviticus 12). It was during their time at the
temple that Simeon's promise from God came true.

The Holy Spirit had revealed to Simeon that before he died, he
would see the Messiah (Jesus, our Savior). The Bible doesn't tell us
how old Simeon was when the Holy Spirit revealed this to him, and
we don't know how old he is in this part of the story. But I can only
imagine the excitement he must have felt in knowing that one day
he would get to see the Messiah that God had promised!

On the day that Mary and Joseph went to the temple courts (as they were to do according to the law), the Holy Spirit stirred inside Simeon, and he felt compelled to go to the temple that day too. When Mary and Joseph brought Jesus into the temple, Simeon knew that this was the Messiah, and he took Jesus into his arms and praised God for sending Jesus, just like He said He would.

I don't know what is stirring in your minds with this story, but here is what I am wondering…

- I wonder if Simeon cried when he took Jesus into his arms because he was so happy to see this promise from God come true?
- I wonder how long he held Jesus?
- I wonder if Jesus cried when Simeon held Him or if He was content and at peace?
- I wonder if Mary and Joseph wondered who this man was that was now holding their child?

I get a few tears in my eyes when I think about Simeon and what this moment must have been like for him. He was holding the Savior of the world. He was rocking God's Son in his arms. He held Jesus and snuggled Him close as he praised God and spoke a blessing over Mary and Joseph. What an amazing day in the life of Simeon, a devout Jewish man, who was promised to see the Son of God before he died. A promise that came true.

Awesome God, thank You for the fulfillment of Your greatest promise: Jesus, our Savior. Amen.

BORN
TO WORSHIP

WONDERING NOTES

* * * * * * * * * * * *

Things I wonder about in this story...

_____

_____

_____

_____

WONDERING SNAPSHOT

Draw a picture of the story

WONDERS TO UNPACK

• • • • • • • • • • • • •

After Simeon praised God, he then spoke directly to Mary and Joseph and prophesied about Jesus. He told them that Jesus would cause both the rise and fall of many people in Israel, that people would not like Jesus, and that Mary would experience much sadness (which she did as she was there when Jesus was crucified).

*Place Day 23
Sticker Here*

24

ANNA SHARES ABOUT JESUS
LUKE 2:36-38

"Coming up to them at that very moment, she gave thanks to God and spoke about the child to all who were looking forward to the redemption of Jerusalem." Luke 2:38

When something amazing happens to you, do you instantly give thanks to God and then share it with someone else?

I am going to go out on a limb here and say that's probably not what you instantly do. I know that I don't. I strive to, but oftentimes I don't thank God at the very moment something happens. It might take me an hour, a day, or maybe even a week to give thanks to God for what He did for me. But I want to make giving thanks a habit, just like the prophet, Anna, did.

Anna was a prophet who spent most of her life in the Jerusalem temple worshiping and praying. She was 84 years old and was a widow (her husband had died many years before). So, she decided to spend her life serving God. The Bible tells us that she fasted and prayed day and night. I'm not sure this actually means she spent every waking minute in the temple, but I do believe she spent every day serving God and worshiping Him.

And in her old age, guess who she got to see while at the temple? She saw Jesus!

While Simeon was in the temple, Anna was also there! At the very moment that Joseph and Mary entered the temple courts, Anna came up to them and began thanking God for Jesus. She knew who this baby was, just like Simeon did! She knew that He was the Savior that God had promised. And she immediately thanked God and went out to spread this news to all. She had to let everyone know that God's promise was here!

Anna is the second person we've read about who shared the Good News with others. Do you remember who the very first people to share about the birth of Jesus were? The shepherds! Both the shepherds and Anna were filled with such wonder and excitement about the arrival of the Savior that they had to go tell other people about Him!

Can you picture this scene in your mind? What are some things you are wondering about?

- I wonder what Anna's reaction was when she saw Mary, Joseph, and Jesus enter the temple? Did she scream, cry, jump up and down, or just stand in awe?
- I wonder if Anna held baby Jesus like Simeon did?
- I wonder if Anna hugged Mary and Joseph?
- I wonder if the people she told about Jesus were in wonder and awe, just like the people the shepherds had told?

When God does amazing things in our lives and blesses us, the first thoughts in our minds and words out of our mouths should be in thanks and praise to Him. Let's work hard to be like Anna, thanking God and telling others what He has done for us.

Awesome God, forgive me when I don't praise You for what You do for me. Help me to remember to always praise You, just like Anna. Amen.

WONDERING NOTES

Things I wonder about in this story...

_____

_____

_____

_____

WONDERING SNAPSHOT

Draw a picture of the story

WONDERS TO UNPACK

Anna could tell people about an experience that not many in the Bible, at least at this time, could say that they had: seeing the Lord Himself. She had seen the physical body of God, who came to the Earth as a baby and would one day die on the cross for our sins so that we can live forever with Him in heaven.

Place Day 24 Sticker Here

SUITCASE STICKERS

Mary and Joseph need some more stickers for their suitcase! In the circles below, create some stickers for their suitcase based on what you have learned about them during Advent.

BONUS DEVOTIONS

Advent officially ends on Christmas Eve. On Christmas Day, we are no longer waiting for or anticipating the birth of Jesus. We celebrate that He has come!

I have included two bonus devotions for you to do. One is for you to read on Christmas Day. Before you open your presents, I highly encourage you and your family to read Luke 2:1-20, along with the Christmas Day devotion in this book. Make Jesus the first thing your family celebrates before tearing into all the presents under the tree.

As we close out the season of Advent, you may be secretly wondering in the back of your mind why I left out an important part of the Christmas story. You may be thinking, "Vanessa, you left out the wise men!" But...the wise men didn't come right away to Bethlehem. Their journey may have actually happened up to two years after the birth of Jesus. The exact time frame isn't certain. So, we don't talk about the story of the wise men during Advent because they entered the scene later. We celebrate their story on Epiphany, which happens twelve days after Christmas Day on January 6th. The second bonus devotion is for you to read on Epiphany (January 6th). On this day, you will celebrate the journey of the wise men to Bethlehem.

Enjoy reading these two bonus devotions involving the birth of Jesus!

IS HE HERE YET?

ISAIAH 9:6-7

"And he will be called Wonderful Counselor, Mighty God, Everlasting Father, Prince of Peace." Isaiah 9:6b

It's Christmas Day! The day you have been so excited to arrive is finally here!

But what is the reason for your excitement? Are you excited because you can't wait to open the presents that have been sitting under your tree all month? Or to look to see what's inside your stocking? Or maybe you're excited to eat a big meal and see all your family?

All of these are things to be excited about! But as Christians, our excitement should first be about celebrating the birth of Jesus. During Advent, we have wondered and waited in anticipation of the arrival of Jesus. But now that Christmas Day is here, is our first focus on Jesus?

700 years before the birth of Jesus, the prophet Isaiah told the Israelites that a child would be born who would be the Messiah. This baby, a Son, would be given to us, and He would be great among all the nations. He would be called "Wonderful Counselor, Mighty God, Everlasting Father, Prince of Peace" (Isaiah 9:6b). He will be King and His kingdom will never end!

Maybe the Israelites thought Isaiah's prophecy would come true right then or maybe sometime later in their lifetime. So, from generation to generation, this prophecy was shared. Parents who were faithful followers of God passed down this foretelling of what was to come to their children and grandchildren. It was the promise of God that He would send a Savior.

They waited and waited and waited.

I can only imagine the thoughts going through the minds of the Israelites over the generations...

- I wonder if they wondered how this was going to come about?
- I wonder if they wondered how they would know which baby would be the Messiah?
- I wonder if any kids kept asking "Is He here yet?"
- I wonder if any of them gave up hope that God would send a Son to save us?
- I wonder if parents told their kids to just be patient?

The Israelites were not always patient or faithful people. We see their lack of patience and faithfulness over and over again throughout the Bible. But Jesus did come...700 years later. God's time is not our time. And sometimes we must wait.

Here's the most amazing thing: God is faithful! His promises never fail. We can know this for sure because of His promise to send His Son to save us. We no longer must wait for a Savior. He is here. Praise be to God!

Thank You, God, for Jesus! Help me to remember Your faithfulness and Your promises. You are Truth and I trust in You. Amen.

WONDERING NOTES

Things I wonder about in this story...

_____

_____

_____

_____

WONDERING SNAPSHOT

Draw a picture of the story

WONDERS TO UNPACK

Jesus is the best gift that you will ever receive. He is a gift for every single person, and the coolest thing is that you can share the gift of Jesus with others by telling them about Him!

*Place
Christmas Day
Sticker Here*

THE STAR HAS RISEN
MATTHEW 2:1-18

"On coming to the house, they saw the child with his mother Mary, and they bowed down and worshiped him. Then they opened their treasures and presented him with gifts of gold, frankincense and myrrh." Matthew 2:11

Have you ever looked up at the sky at night and noticed the beautiful stars? If you have, you will have noticed that there are so many stars in the sky. Ever tried to count them? There are too many to count! Some shine brightly, while others are a little dimmer. I love looking up on a clear night to see the dazzling stars in the sky.

There were men at this time in history who studied the stars and the cosmic events behind them. In the book of Matthew, we see that these men are called Magi, but we also call them wise men.

These Magi had journeyed from the East because they saw a very bright and shining star in the sky. Seeing this, they knew that the King of the Jews had been born and they wanted to worship Him. After making a pit stop in Jerusalem to learn more information, they found out that the King of the Jews had been born in Bethlehem.

When they left Jerusalem, the star guided them directly to the place where Mary and Joseph were staying. And there they worshiped Jesus and gave Him gifts of gold, frankincense, and myrrh.

While our Nativity scenes today show three Magi with Mary and Joseph in the stable (or cave), that's not where the Magi actually found them. Mary and Joseph had made their way from the cave to a home in Bethlehem, and it was here that the wise men were guided by the star (Matthew 2:11). We are not exactly sure of the time frame, but based on Matthew 2:16, it could have been up to two years after the birth of Jesus when they found Him.

Does this reality have your mind wondering a little bit? Here's what I am wondering about...

- I wonder how long it took the Magi to travel to Bethlehem?
- I wonder if they had ever seen a star like this before?
- I wonder how much gold, frankincense, and myrrh they gave to Jesus?
- I wonder what Mary and Joseph did with these gifts?
- I wonder if Mary and Joseph were surprised by this visit from men they did not know who came to give them gifts?

God sent a very bright star in the sky to guide the Magi to Jesus. Today, Jesus is our shining light. We follow Him, as He is our guide and the One who will lead us in the direction we need to go. Keep following the light of Jesus!

Holy God, when life gets hard, help me to see the light of Jesus and to keep following You. Amen.

WONDERING NOTES

● ● ● ● ● ● ● ● ● ● ● ●

Things I wonder about in this story...

_____

_____

_____

_____

WONDERING SNAPSHOT

Draw a picture of the story

WONDERS TO UNPACK

Our tradition says that there were three Magi. We don't know this for sure, but we base this assumption on the number of gifts that were given to baby Jesus (the three gifts of gold, frankincense, and myrrh). There could have been three Magi, but there also could have been a lot more!

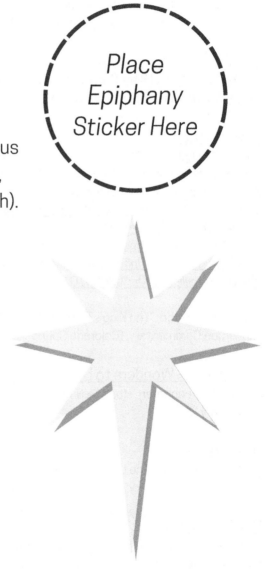

Place Epiphany Sticker Here

NOTES

Day Nine - Wonders to Unpack
[1] Warren Wiersbe, "The King's Birth," in Matthew-Galatians, Vol. 1 of The Bible Exposition Commentary, (Colorado Springs: David C. Cook, 1989), 14.

Day Ten - Wonders to Unpack
[2] The Chronological Bible (New International Version), "Betrayal and Betrothal", (Nashville: Thomas Nelson, 2014), 1092.

Day Fourteen
[3] Stella U. Ogunwole, Megan A. Rabe, Andrew W. Roberts, and Zoe Caplan, "U.S. Adult Population Grew Faster Than Nation's Total Population From 2010 to 2020," Resource Library, United States Census Bureau, published August 12, 2021, https://www.census.gov/library/stories/2021/08/united-states-adult-population-grew-faster-than-nations-total-population-from-2010-to-2020.html#:~:text=Population%20Under%20Age%2018%20Declined%20Last%20Decade&text=In%202020%2C%20the%20U.S.%20Census,from%20234.6%20million%20in%202010.

[4] Warren Wiersbe, "The King's Birth," in Matthew-Galatians, Vol. 1 of The Bible Exposition Commentary, (Colorado Springs: David C. Cook, 1989), 175.

Day Fifteen - Wonders to Unpack
[5] Beth Guckenberger, "Hope Defined," (Children's Pastors Conference, Orlando, FL, January 2023).

Day Sixteen
[6] Warren Wiersbe, "The Lord is Come," in Matthew-Galatians, Vol. 1 of The Bible Exposition Commentary, (Colorado Springs: David C. Cook, 1989), 176.

Day Seventeen
[7] Warren Wiersbe, "The Lord is Come," in Matthew-Galatians, Vol. 1 of The Bible Exposition Commentary, (Colorado Springs: David C. Cook, 1989), 176.

NOTES

Day Eighteen - Wonders to Unpack

[8] Warren Wiersbe, "The Lord is Come," in Matthew-Galatians, Vol. 1 of The Bible Exposition Commentary, (Colorado Springs: David C. Cook, 1989), 176.

ACKNOWLEDGMENTS

I have always wanted to write a devotional for kids that is centered around the Christmas story, and I am so grateful to God for giving me the idea of using our wonder and imagination to think deeper about the birth of Jesus. All glory and honor go to Him.

Thank you to my family for always supporting me in every book I write or idea I have in helping kids learn the Bible and grow in their faith. Sometimes my ideas are big, and my husband, children, parents, sisters, and in-laws are always there cheering me on and encouraging me along the way.

Thank you to my friend (and associate pastor at my church), Rev. Robin Parr, for reading this devotional ahead of time and guiding me in the Word.

May God bless all of you as you read His Word and grow closer to Him this Advent season.

ABOUT THE AUTHOR

Vanessa Myers has a passion for helping families build faith that lasts for generations. She is a children's minister, author, speaker, and founder of Family Faith Builders, LLC. She creates simple Bible resources for families that help kids dig into God's Word in fun and engaging ways. Check out her resources and books on her website: www.familyfaithbuilders.org

Hey Parents! Connect with Vanessa on Social Media:

Facebook: familyfaithbuilders22
Instagram: familyfaithbuilders
Pinterest: familyfaithbuilders22

START YOUR DAY WITH JESUS!

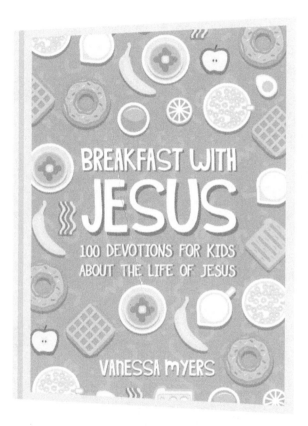

A book that helps kids come to know Jesus through reading His Word and following Him!

Available on Amazon!

Made in United States
North Haven, CT
14 November 2023

44002411R00075